MANKIND ENCOUNTERING ANGELS IN POETRY OF IQBAL

Khurram Ellahi

AURAQ

Printed in the Islamic Republic of Pakistan.
First Printed: July, 2019
ISBN: 978-969-7868-15-5
Price: Rs 600 PKR, 6$ USD

AURAQ
PUBLICATIONS
ISLAMABAD, PAKISTAN

raabta@auraqpublications.com.pk | +92-300-0571-530
www.auraqpublications.com.pk | @AuraqPublications
ISBN : 978-969-7868-15-5

Dedicated to:
Ahmed Javaid sb

Acknowledgements

My first book i.e. *Managers as Little Prince* invited readers to look at the dilemmas of the world with an eye of a poet. We used fiction and poetry as a guiding tool for sciences and precisely for Management Science. In that book, I dedicated a chapter to the existential conditions of Man. Specifically, man at workplace. Being an ardent reader of Iqbal, I wanted to take Iqbal's view on "How Man struggles to survive in this universe while keeping the balance between reality and idealism". Thus, I had to look around me. How so many lives completed me. How their sacrifices gave strength to me which is similar to story of Man, who has been martyred for creation of this world. Man who bears all pain and worries to live another day. If there is no Man, material world would lose its meaning, too. But to be the active consciousness of the world, Man has paid a heavy price. I guess, so did I.

My Father has kept me away from single morsel of corrupted income which gives me strength to walk the toughest of paths, strengthens me to never take a shortcut. I imagine myself to be a father like him, his presence makes me secure in toughest of times. What else is father for. My philosophical development started from the lunch which I used to have after school at home. My Mother would tell us tales from Quran and would allow us to participate fully in it. My mother's prayers are the virtual defense shield which I carried in life; I feel my all lucky bounties appeared because of her prayers. I have no idea how one lives without parents. This book attends this issue; first we are bound to love them and later we leave them. Forever. A kid is never taught in life how to live without parents but we take the risk, we live another day with the dream that we will never be apart.

Shaheer, my eldest brother impregnated my brain with whole world of ideas. He astonishes you every day with a new dimension. How could you not be intelligent while living with him. Hamza, my elder brother gave me all the support so that I could believe in idealism. So I could stay another night in a dream of utopia. Thank you, Apa & Sonia, for all little support I can never forget.

Shah Hussain & Banujah taught me the balance between heart & reason. While one is all love and other is beyond reason. But I guess they both are all love. Proudly, Hussain is growing up now and he can read these lines. Aleyah & Waleyah, whenever you read this line, remember to never let a night go when you don't read. Wife, thank you for bearing me. Told you; it isn't easy marrying a philosopher.

Shehryar Afridi has practically told me that fame is nothing. Never run for it. He guided me that travel as long as you can to meet a sage. If you ever get impressed by someone, get impressed from the trait of intelligence. Dr. Hassan Rasool has reasonably manifested me that how I may act in the world once I am acknowledged as a scholar.

To all Readers out there; Read, Read & Read before the words disappear. Before we are left on mercy of algorithms. Cry, cry & cry before there are no more sorrows in this universe. Before future is all predictable, before uncertainties are reduced into numbers and machines win all. Read.

Contents

Mankind Encountering Angels in Poetry of Iqbal

Since antiquity, mankind had been fantasized by supernatural beings. Looking at Greek, Norse or Indian mythology, we find myriad of figures which were used by mankind to create their link with God. May it be Huginn & Muninn, two ravens receiving all the news for Odin or List of demi-gods and lower-gods who use to run affairs for Zeus and performing various tasks for Him.

Though the Satan of Islam is considered to be an entity made of fire, yet Satan was also considered to be the Angel who had access in court of God and he brought the climax to the story of Adam & Eve. Zoroastrianism is also captivated by the idea of Angels. Amesha Spentas, which are seven divine attributes, are also regarded as Angels for Ahura Mazda. However, Zoroastrianism also carries the idea of guardian angel called Fravashi.

Literature is also under the charm of Angels. We have poems to stage-plays revolving around

Angels. *Dr. Faustus* by Christopher Marlowe reflects how mankind struggles between the voices of Good & Evil spirits. On the contrary, in "His Dark Materials", Philip Pullman defends the case of rebel spirits, who taught mankind to be creative and not submissive. The famous work of Blake "The Angel" still mesmerizes many by creating a relationship between Man and Angel.

Abrahamic religions have left a great discussion on Angels. Even in holy texts and also in words of Prophets. However, as this book looks at encounter between Man and Angel in poetry of Iqbal, it is exceedingly important to look at a verse of Quran which, as per Muslim text, highlights the first encounter between Archetype Man and Angels.

As the current book will look into poetry of Iqbal and how Iqbal built an empire of argument, while resting on same verse of Quran.

Quran in its chapter 2 verse 30 quotes:

وَإِذْ قَالَ رَبُّكَ لِلْمَلَٰٓئِكَةِ إِنِّي جَاعِلٌ فِى ٱلْأَرْضِ خَلِيفَةً قَالُوٓا۟ أَتَجْعَلُ فِيهَا مَن يُفْسِدُ فِيهَا وَيَسْفِكُ ٱلدِّمَآءَ وَنَحْنُ نُسَبِّحُ بِحَمْدِكَ وَنُقَدِّسُ لَكَ قَالَ إِنِّىٓ أَعْلَمُ مَا لَا تَعْلَمُونَ ۝

"And [mention, O Muhammad], when your Lord said to the angels, "Indeed, I will make upon the earth a successive authority." They said, "Will You place upon it one who causes corruption therein and sheds blood, while we declare Your praise and sanctify You?" Allah said, "Indeed, I know that which you do not know."

Then Allah, the Creator of man and angels, further added in next verse:

وَعَلَّمَ ءَادَمَ ٱلْأَسْمَآءَ كُلَّهَا ثُمَّ عَرَضَهُمْ عَلَى ٱلْمَلَٰٓئِكَةِ فَقَالَ أَنۢبِـُٔونِى بِأَسْمَآءِ هَٰٓؤُلَآءِ إِن كُنتُمْ صَٰدِقِينَ ۝

"And He taught Adam the names - all of them. Then He showed them to the angels and said, "Inform Me of the names of these, if you are truthful."

Allah, the Creator of Man and Angels, taught mankind language, names, nouns, rhetoric, prose, and poem to stand against the hardest of the winds of universe. Iqbal used the same. Iqbal used language to build his thesis, to make man again the center of universe, to make man again the most-supreme creation of Allah. Iqbal chose poetry.

Thus, current book will leap into poetry of Iqbal to see how Iqbal put thesis of Man in front of world in comparison to Angels.

Three Archangels are considered to be holy and imperative part of Catholic Church. Those are Michael (AS), Gabriel (AS), and Raphael (AS). In Islam, which reflects itself as a continuity and finality of Abrahamic Religions, these angels are considered to be the part of Six Articles of Faith. Names of Gabriel (AS), Michel (AS), and Raphael (AS) are repeatedly found in Muslim Text. Name of Gabriel even appears in Quran and Gabriel appeared with first revelation to

Prophet Muhammad (ﷺ).

However, man still remains as the Caliph and vicegerent of God in universe as per the philosophy of Iqbal. This narrative was weakening up in time of Iqbal. At secular ends with the dawn of Darwinism, clubbed with existentialism, it was found that man is a chance-being having no meaning or essence. Man was found to be irrelevant to where cosmos is heading. On the other hand in religious camps, Man was placed as a toy in hands of God mediated by Angels. Iqbal, being a genius from sub-continent, had the chance to read the best of secular works while rooting him in religious land. He had to see and encounter the texts from both of ends. It could be seen in Iqbal's poetry as he was on a mission to liberate Man from the chains of modern absurdism, and also actualizing Man's place in Holy world by freeing Man from fear of Angels. Iqbal addresses God's relationship to man with the verse of Quran:

وَلَقَدْ خَلَقْنَا ٱلْإِنسَـٰنَ وَنَعْلَمُ مَا تُوَسْوِسُ بِهِۦ نَفْسُهُۥ ۖ وَنَحْنُ أَقْرَبُ إِلَيْهِ مِنْ حَبْلِ ٱلْوَرِيدِ

(٢٩)

"And We have already created man and know what his soul whispers to him, and We are closer to him than [his] jugular vein." (50:16)

This book is an attempt to re-identify the role of mankind in God's universe. As Iqbal himself is more interested to know "what is man and how man is the highest being in God's universe". Reading Urdu text of Iqbal, so many couplets of Iqbal are found challenging or debating with Archangels that I took on a little journey to compile a book on this issue.

Iqbal is extremely interested to know the position of man, role of man and how man stands taller than any other being. Iqbal has a magic to put anti-thesis of a religious understanding through higher religious references. Iqbal helps man to transcend nearer to God by putting anti-thesis to established-understanding of religion. Famous lectures of Iqbal even have a title of "Reconstruction of Religious Thoughts in Islam". "Reconstruction" is like a newer thesis but still rooting itself in fundamentals of religious text of Islam.

Hence, Iqbal considered a dire need that Man may relocate his position and sit on the throne again to lead the cosmos. One of major barriers that traditional Mullah created in way was Angels; Man became a slave under the eyes of Angels. For Iqbal, result was visible when sub-continent was enslaved by East India Company. Man has created a veil between him and God in name of Angels.

With the decline of religious narratives and rise of Humanism, religious scholars had to look into newer meaning for Man, they had to tag man with novel reason in this universe. As Humanism made man best by possibly-available and acknowledging man's pain while living the experience of life.

Looking into work of Iqbal, we see Iqbal going through a lot. Reconstruction was one major attempt to reconstitute Man's position in world. Specifically, in Islamic context. Which was long lost. Hence, we see Iqbal writing about WILL, Knowledge, Religious Experience in his book *Reconstruction of Religious Thoughts in Islam*. With that he corrects role of man in world. Liberating man to be mere puppet in hands of natural forces, Iqbal had to reinvent the answer while staying in line with words of Muslim religious scripture. Hence in poetry, Iqbal introduced this concept so it can be digested by religious scholars.

Embarking on the journey to explore how Iqbal puts forward the thesis of Man in front of universe in his book *Gabriel Wing*, let's start the journey from first poem of his book *Armaghaan-e-Hijaaz* (The Gift of Hijaaz). Title of the poem

The Devil's Conference has attraction for both secular & non-secular minds. First verse is:

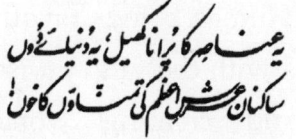

"This ancient game of elements, this base world! The frustration of the longings of the great Empyrean's dwellers."

Which reflects that God has already turned down the whims of nearby dwellers of His throne and created Man. This takes us back to Quran's chapter The Cow verse 30:

"Angels: "Will You place upon it one who causes corruption therein and sheds blood, while we declare Your praise and sanctify You?"

Allah replied in same verse to Angels *"Indeed, I know that which you do not know."*

Iqbal has given explanation for same verse from new dimension. Reflecting that words and wishes of Angels were not approved. Declined by the Supreme Authority of the universe, highlighting in Quran that wisdom of Angels is not holistic. Human beings, on other hand, have been blessed with the gift of wisdom, an art of inquiring and creating wonders through knowledge which gives them an exalted position among all beings created by Allah.

Iqbal has created a link of this verse in his poetic work by introducing a newer term that whims and desires of Angels were declined in front of existence of Man.

This verse, as used by Iqbal, refers to the beginning of the Man's journey. And reflects that first doubt on Man's creation was casted by Angels. Iqbal is late to show the competition or Iqbal is late to exalt the position of Man. As referred by Quran, Angels considered Man to be reason of quarrel and fights on earth. Hence Iqbal being honest to the race of Man, created a link with this verse and empowered Man to be more active in universe with mastery of words and wisdom as gifted by Allah.

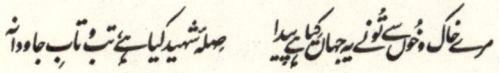

"Out of my flesh and blood You made this earth;
Its quenchless fever the martyr's crown of gold."

Iqbal highlights again that this cosmos has existed on cost of Man's existential condition. As rest of the creations are passive, non-living things or matter in motion. Only man is going through the crisis of psychology and his existence. All other creations or beings are enjoying their static or pre-destined roles. Only man has taken on universe and he is adding colors on cost of his entropic life. A life in which he decays each moment yet keep on adding new colors to the dark world around him. Iqbal ends the verse with the dream that in Quran the Martyr has been promised with eternal life. Almighty, human race should be awarded with eternal life as Man is the only Martyr on scale of all beings. Universe is made out of flesh and blood of feeble Man, who appears on this Earth for a span of few years and in those few years he has to find the ultimate truth while also succeeding in petty affairs of daily life. By earning bread to sustain his body and by approaching prayers to sustain his soul, yet knowing that nothing is eternal. He is disappearing every moment. With each day Man as a pencil erases himself to give an extra line to this universe. As Almighty made Man against the whim of Angels, yet Man also took all the pain so the journey of this universe may not stop. With feeble body, Man continues the ride.

As per Freudian psychology, man's psychology has three main parts: ID, Ego and Super-ego. In all major religious text, a system of sin and virtue runs. Mankind is offered a cannon to follow. If they follow that and stay away from harmful acts, they are considered to be pious and revered in front of Divinity. But if they don't follow the *Dos* and *Don'ts* list of religion, they are considered to be sinful.

But moving to the story of Adam & Eve, which is accepted with minor changes in Abrahamic religions, the story of mankind started after a mistake or a sin committed by first Prophet i.e., Adam (AS). Almighty directed Adam & Eve not to eat from that particular tree. But as they were the bearer of free-will, they couldn't resist and on the bait of Satan they went to eat that fruit against the will of Almighty. Christianity particularly calls this event as original sin.

تاخسار فرشتے نذركے آبا   قصوروازغریب اللّدیارٌہوں سکین

"I am at "fault", and in a foreign land,
But the angels never could make habitable that
wasteland of yours."

Iqbal has used the word "fault" and tried to encompass the original sin associated with mankind. Here, Iqbal refers that though we, as mankind, are at fault, sinful, and guilty, yet mankind has given the colors to this mute universe. Iqbal further called planet Earth as wasteland and added that Angels never made this universe habitable. This planet Earth is full of life, having sin & virtues due to mankind and if this responsibility was given to Angels that could have been disappointment. As Man is the only carrier of free-will, colors, arts, and science. Giving a larger meaning to the universe. Rest if invested on Angels, they couldn't have made this universe habitable. Certainly, here Iqbal refers to Man as the driving force which has energy to make planets livelier. Though man has an ID in him, which makes him vulnerable to go astray, still the passion of Man has made planet Earth a central point of universe.

Next couplet of same poem further adds light on Iqbal's view of Angels:

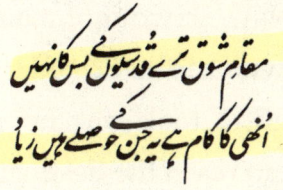

"The station of love is beyond the reach of Your angels,
Only those of dauntless courage are up to it."

Here, Iqbal puts forward his request to Almighty that Angels can't bear this journey of passion and love. It is only the courage of Man that he embarked on this journey of passion. Passion as shown by Christ in his last moments, Hussain (RA) showed that passion in Karbala, Muhammad (ﷺ) showed that passion while stones were casted on him, when garbage was thrown on him, when bed linings left marks on his body every night. Yet they stood for the name of Almighty. Hence for Iqbal, courage of man is much higher than supernatural beings i.e. Angels. Thus, Iqbal reflected that journey of passion was never for Angels. The height of love would always stay out of reach of Angels, however Man who has dedicated his life for the love of Almighty, took all the pain in the journey so he can reach the destination; God.

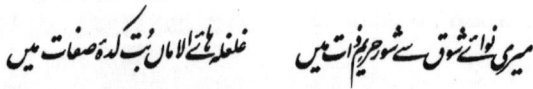

"My epiphany of passion causes commotion in the precinct of the Divine Essence,
Strikes terror in the pantheon of His Attributes."

My longing, my lament, my poetry has reached the Throne of God and has created a movement in the holy sphere (not accessible to any creation of God). Not only Throne of God but uproar is also shaking the foundation of Earth (which is nothing but a home of attributes of God). Reflecting that poetry of man, based on his existential conditions in life, can reach the height where no angel can reach. Lament of Man powered with right passion for his Creator can reach the most private zones of this universe.

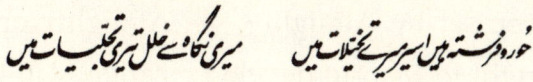

"The houri and the angel are captives of my imaginations –
My glance ruffles Your Manifestations."

Iqbal further adds that Angel and *Hur* are nothing but ideas dwelling in Man's consciousness. Hence, Man's consciousness is the deepest and widest place of the universe. All realities, ideas, and empirical facts are held there. Angels are nothing but ideas drawn on canvas of Man's consciousness. No object can exist until it is observed by only active phenomenon of this universe i.e. Man. Man is the subject which makes all existences real and understandable. Thus, may it be *Hur* or Angels, they are captivated in human brain. Man is the subject which makes all possibilities and ideas possible. While completing the verse, Iqbal further adds that sight of Perfect Man can change the design of universe, the design which has been set by Almighty, yet Almighty only gave right to Man to develop creative plan for this universe.

عشق کی اک جست نے طے کردیا قصہ تمام   اس زمین و آسمان کو بے کراں سمجھا تھا میں

"One leap by Love ended all the pother,
I fondly imagined, the earth and sky were
boundless."

It is assumed or believed that Angels are supernatural beings with special powers. As earlier discussed, either they are in Abrahamic religions, Norse Mythology or in Arts, wings are attached to this entity which reflects their strength to travel in skies. Looking at grand universe around us, flying has always been the strength which mankind envy for. Scientifically speaking, we are living in infinitely huge universe, out of which a very small proportion is only explored. Hubble telescope even loses its powers to see in deep areas of universe. Yet myths and religious literature believe that Angels can travel with great speed within this universe. We know that even speed of light is too slow to travel the distances of this vast universe. Angels with wings reflect their power to travel distances and to show their control over aisles within the skies.

However, Iqbal again introduces Man as the only one to encompass universe. Referring to Prophet Muhammad's (ﷺ) journey of Miraj, Iqbal highlights that infinite universe has been traveled within split seconds with the power of passion and love. With fuel of love, Man has traveled with speed even anonymous to Angels. Love has given access to areas which are unknown to Angels. Here Iqbal suggests to all other existences and also to naive men crawling on earth, that universe you consider to be infinite is nothing but covered in a leap by Man of love and wisdom.

سبق پڑھے پیہ معراج مصطفیٰؐ سے مجھے   کہ عالمِ بشریت کی زد میں ہے گردوں

"By Holy Prophet (ﷺ)'s Ascent this truth to me was taught,
Within the reach of man high heavens can be brought."

Iqbal, in his work *Reconstruction of Religious Thoughts in Islam*, further interpreted the philosophy of Miraj of Prophet Muhammed (ﷺ). Miraj is a mystic journey in which Prophet Muhammed (ﷺ) travelled from planet Earth to beyond seven skies and met Almighty - the Creator of all. However, there is a catch in this mystic journey, while other Prophets specifically Moses (AS) wanted to meet Allah, wanted to see him in Real, Muhammed (ﷺ) never desired for same yet Almighty privileged him with this honor. Moses (AS) kept saying that I want to see, and Almighty replied that you can't see Me. As Moses (AS) was missing an important point that in order to meet Allah, he wouldn't have to leave humans and people down here; who're still living a life of ignorance.

On other hand, Muhammad (ﷺ) kept living in society, worked on reforms, brought behavioral changes in community and would always dedicate his nights in remembering Allah. Hence, Allah privileged Prophet Muhammad (ﷺ) with an invitation to see Him, to be the one meeting Him in absolute timelessness, at absolute space. However, for Iqbal, highest lesson of Miraj is Moral.

Iqbal has reflected this act as height of Humanism, even when Divine was in front of Muhammad (ﷺ), Prophet Muhammad (ﷺ) came down to attend the sorrows of Mankind. Iqbal further added that Miraj has left us with a lesson that Man's earth is the center of universe, Man's earth is central attraction for Divine. This again is a silent message for other creations and existences.

As added by Iqbal:

عروج آدمِ خاکی سے انجم سہمے جاتے ہیں
کہ یہ ٹوٹا ہوا تارا مہِ کامل نہ بن جائے

"The rise of clay-born man hath smit the hosts of heaven with utter fright: They dread that this fallen star to moon may wax with fuller light."

خودی ہو علم سے محکم تو غیرتِ جبریل   اگر ہو عشق سے محکم تو صورِ اسرافیل

"If self with knowledge strong becomes, Gabriel it can envious make:
If fortified with passion great, Like trump of Israfil can shake."

Khudi i.e. highest point of self-realization or Ego is the central concept of Iqbal's philosophy. It's like realizing who created me, I am touched by the will of God who is infinite, eternal, omnipotent and omnipresent. Khudi helps Man to acknowledge his place in the ephemeral world. World only exists because it is observed by eyes of the Man, interpreted by the mind of the Man, it has colors and rainbow due to romanticism of Man. Else, it's nothing but a weak land of clay, jumbled up with mountains and water running. Man's existence provides it with the meaning. Thus, Khudi raises mankind from being mere biological existences. Khudi transcends mankind and authorizes Man to be the only carrier of Divine Will.

In this couplet, Iqbal highlights that if Man achieves Khudi through knowledge and wisdom, then certainly Gabriel (AS) (one of Archangels in Islam) would take pride in knowing Man. Gabriel (AS) would cherish existence of Man. Realizing Khudi through knowledge is not the only way. In next phrase, Iqbal further elaborates that if Khudi is actualized through love and passion then Khudi, as instrument, can be as powerful as Israfil's (Raphael AS) trumpet. Israfil (Raphael AS) holds a very sacred position in Islam.

Israfil's (AS) trumpet-blowing will be signal for resurrection. Thus, reflecting that Israfil's (AS) trumpet would raise dead ones again from the graves. Dead ones would get another life before day of judgment by the will of this trumpet's sound. Iqbal refers to Khudi as a tool, as powerful as Israfil's trumpet, which can raise the dead ones again. Thus, humans once acknowledging their real position in this world, can raise dead souls again. Iqbal's major aim is to highlight that words of great sages, speeches of great men can give life to dead nations and can change their fate which is as valuable as having a life on day of resurrection.

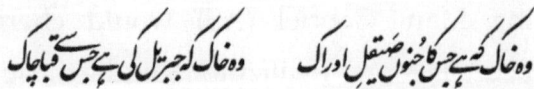

"That frantic dust whose eye outranges reason, Dust by whose madness Gabriel's rose is rent."

Man is usually called as dust or sand by Iqbal. Man has been designed by dust as explained in Holy Quran:

وَلَقَدْ خَلَقْنَا ٱلْإِنسَٰنَ مِن سُلَٰلَةٍ مِّن طِينٍ ﴿١٢﴾

"And certainly, did We create man from an extract of clay."

Iqbal, being poet, is also highlighting another important point that Man lives on clay or the land which is the adobe made of clay. Poet, metaphorically, divides two important dimensions of the universe; *Khaaki* as denizens of land and *Aflaaki* as divine entities who dwell in skies. Thus, Man is made of clay and dwells in adobe made up of clay. Flying, raising himself up from clay, dreaming of travelling the Milky Way or harboring skies have been a long dream of Man. Yet due to the body under which Man appears on Earth, this looks like a lucid dream only. But the passion, a spark of passion makes Man immortal. Reason of Man once finding fuel from passion of heart makes Gabriel (AS) wonder on this vulnerable Man. Iqbal completes the couplet by adding the name of Archangel Gabriel (AS); Man's wisdom,

39

added up with passion, can torn up the veil of Gabriel. It's only with mankind that even they know that the task is impossible, yet they will never reduce the effort. This is the Grand Tragedy of mankind. Reason has worked out that bird has flown away, yet the passion is looking for it with madness. That madness will find the way to truth beyond rationality. Thus, Iqbal again echoes here with his earlier thought that Man has been blessed with rationality and passion together and using them wisely; the veil or the veil of Angels can be removed to see Reality.

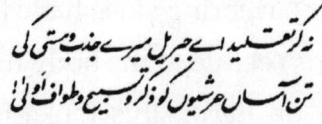

"O Gabriel (AS) do not follow my absorption and enthusiasm

For trouble free sky creatures, it's better to do prayers, count beads and go round."

Iqbal cherished the ecstasy of mankind throughout his poetry. Material universe is static, encaged by the innate roles, performing the predetermined role, heading to abyss with utmost silence. Then we have the mankind. Man, who does poetry, who writes plays, who roams wildly in search of loved-one, who walks hardest roads knowing that his beloved is on another end. How Ibraheem (AS) was thrown into fire yet he came out smiling, how Moses (AS) walked through the sea while others were left astonished, how Jesus (AS) was raised on the cross yet he didn't utter a word against the will of God. Ecstasy, which was reflected by Sufi poets by writing magic through pen. Showing a world beyond rationality, opening doors of world beyond determinism. Ecstasy, as shown by Hussain (RA) by sacrificing his family against the forces of a tyrant. All these acts were the acts where passion guided the present body rather than the brain. All these acts, if left on brain, would have been declined by body. But passion, rapture, ecstasy guided these great men and made them immortal. This ecstasy floated great work of art & literature, of music & trance from the pen of mortal men. Passion & emotions differentiate me not only from Angels but also from Robots and Artificial Intelligence. Though Robots are master of rationality, complex computing and what not. But we know the amazing art of losing, crying, struggling, and living with grand tragedies. Life is an ephemeral experience where I am conscious of my life yet heading to death is the tragedy which moves me further. Once I have tasted ecstasy, I do miracles which normal brain would never allow me to do.

Here Iqbal called on Gabriel (AS) and asked Gabriel (AS) not to copy the passion and rapture of mankind. Essence of passion, which made Man the dearest creation of God. Which exalted Man from dust to vicegerent of God. Which made Man the bearer of Original sin, yet his tears and repentance gave him access to closest circles of God. Though Man is distant from God, yet Allah calls upon Man in Quran as:

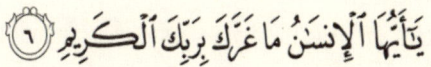

"O mankind, what has deceived you concerning your Lord, the Generous"

This again reflects that God, Creator of all existences, is calling on mankind; what have deceived you, what have kept you away from the Lord. Thus, Iqbal further calls upon Gabriel (AS) that no other form of being can copy the feats of mankind. No other being can reproduce the miracles as performed by Prophets. Angels are trouble-free beings of God. They neither walk through the tight aisles of economics nor have social, political, religious pressures. They are free from all these choices. They are free from the crisis that a Man bears in this life. Hence, Iqbal called Angels as Free-From-Trouble-Existence. On other hand, Man has a body to carry, which hosts illness, Man carries a brain which hosts doubts, Man carries a soul which longs for Creator, and Man as conscious-being; bears that all, live through that all. He picks himself up every day and fulfills all the promises he made with God while living in a weak body. Thus, Iqbal further adds that Angels can only perform prayers and count beads of God's praise. Man does same too but with all the pressures of life, from looking at his own life decaying in front of him, fulfilling economic goals, taking care of neighbor and a list of items that an Angel never has to do. Hence, Iqbal added that prayer of Man is an actual prayer to God, as it is carried against all the whims, wishes, and pressure of life.

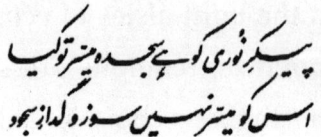

"Celestial beings, born of light, Do have the privilege of supplication, But unknown to them are the verve and warmth of prostration."

What is Man's life? As Vincent said, sadness will last forever. We decay. Birth is the birth of death. Our body is a feeble tool to hold the most powerful soul. Then we have to earn the bread. We have to earn every moment, next hour, day, year. Capitalism has left us as mere consumers. I think therefore I am, is changing as I earn therefore I am; I buy therefore I am. The weak body carries the soul from home to work. And then, there is a call from Lord. Five times a day, muslims need to pray, which is like answering the call from God. Though he is nearer than jugular vein, yet a dedicated time has to be given.

The dilemma here is again existential. My life is like a collection of miseries. Life is like imperfections placed perfectly. I am carrying the load of history along with presence. And with each moment, I am heading to death. Moreover, same God creates my worldly bond of passion with family and love. And life becomes like a scented garden. Life makes meaning for the first time. Later, Man realizes that it was worst of a crisis. They all are slipping away, too. They decay too, as they are humans.

With that, I hear the call for prayer. And leaving all what I was doing for survival, for another day, to earn another moment, else my kids could starve, my mother could leave next medicine, I am called for prayer and I run to the mosque. To Answer. To reply.

Angels are always praying to God and reciting holy names but here Iqbal reflects an ecstatic thought that Angels would never know that how we bow down with heart full of sadness, how we stand in front of Allah while we leave our beloved mother in hospital, how we bow down while our kids wait for next meal, how we bow down while with empty pockets I gave hope to my kids for toys, how I bow down while my mother thinks I will bring her medicine, how I bow down while my father waits that his son will return with some perks. Certainly, it's the Man who caries that all and yet be available to God. Though Angels are always in prayer and reciting verses yet it's the Man whose single utterance of Divine name will delay the day of resurrection. Until single man utters the Holy promise, the universe will exist.

In last part of the book, we will look into message of Angels for mankind. Message which was given in words of Iqbal before Man embarked for mundane journey. However, this complete poem is an actual encounter of Angels and mankind. Looking at Angels' reaction while they observe passionate men, men of honor, men with arts, men who can love, men who can give their life for the God (Martyr), men who wake up from warm night and stand in remembrance of God, men who leave the charm of life, men who consider matter as an illusion and crave for absence.

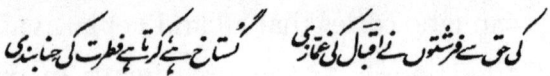

"To God the angels did complain gainst Iqbal and did say
That rude and insolent is he, Nature he paints much brightly."

Angels took complaint of Iqbal in front of God. Angels grieved against the passion of Iqbal. They further added that Iqbal is making this universe more meaningful. He is adding to colors of this universe. He is making universe more attractive by exploring the depth of the universe. Iqbal is enlightening mankind about the mystery of universe. He is urging mankind to decipher the codes of universe to make it more useful for its denizens. Angels (as the word used by Iqbal in verse) called Iqbal as insolent. Iqbal is romanticizing about the role of Man in universe. Iqbal is assigning Man's role as co-creator in the universe, to complete this Divine endeavour of God. Thus, Angel carried this complaint against Iqbal as an archetype of mortal kind.

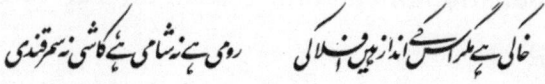

"Though born of mud and water, yet a god assumes to be:
Not bound to any home or land, of earthly ties is free."

Angels further elaborated the case against Iqbal in front of God by highlighting the major offence, of what he is doing in worldly life. He is made up of dust and clay; mere mortal being, yet he aims to be co-creator, vicegerent of the Divine. Being on Earth they idealize infinity, and being mortal; they dream of immortality. Their design is mortal and of dust, yet Man is aiming to be a lord of skies. He is a free soul. Neither is he Roman, Syrian, a man from Samarkand or any other part of the world. Reflecting that man is boundless, his energy can't be captivated. He is a traveler, having no worldly origin. As Man, he looks at his origin in skies from where he landed on Earth. Angels further strengthened the case of offence by next couplet:

سکھلائی فرشتوں کو آدم کی تڑپ اس نے   آدم کو سکھاتا ہے آدابِ خداوندی

"To throngs of Heaven he has taught, like man, to fret and pine. To clay-made man he fain would teach the wont and mode divine."

Here Angels agree that Iqbal has taught us about the pain of the Man. Angels confessed that Iqbal has taught us about the existential crisis of Man. Iqbal has showed us the mirror in which painful life of Man was reflecting. Iqbal has projected the tragic life of Man while living away from the source, while breathing away from his Creator. Living at a distance of thousands of light-years from their God, longing for a meeting, longing for a conversation with the God. Sadly, neither there is a meeting nor a voice of God which lonely

Man can find in abyss. Resulting, Man's life is full of pain and struggle. Pain, to carry the loads of economics, history, health, decay etc. Man, as specie, struggles every second for survival, else we all would disappear. Thus, Iqbal has unveiled this secret of passion and pain of Man on Angels. Angels, who have never tasted this ecstatic phenomenon of passion. But this isn't the only unveiling which Iqbal did. Iqbal has also shown the elixir to mankind, Iqbal has found the panacea to all miseries, sadness, and pain of mankind. As Iqbal has taught Angels about the passion and pain of mankind, similarly Iqbal is teaching Man about the attributes of God and how Man can adopt those attributes to be free from sword of Damocles i.e. Death.

Iqbal has taken inspiration from a famous saying in Arabic:

تخلقوابأخلاق الله

"Believers may adopt the attributes of God."

51

Iqbal has hinted that Man can be free from all pain and suffering by adopting the Divine attributes. Once Man will be intoxicated in ecstasy of Divine attributes, he will free himself from worldly stresses and pressures. Rather Man will look at totality and would work on soul rather than body. As soul is the Divine spark in our body. Soul is the only touch of Divine in this carrier of dust. Thus, by working on soul, we can be free from fear of death and losing our body. This poem is like a climax of encounter which is the primary subject of current book. Rest of the couplets quoted are thesis of mankind that how they are trying to be free from worldly existence which is more like an unasked punishment. This poem is a reply by Angels in which they are advocating a case against Iqbal who is sharing the secrets of Man with Angels. Further sharing the secret of Divine attributes with mankind. Thus, Iqbal is liberating the Man, Angels and all other forms of existences. Iqbal is making us all free by unveiling the secrets of "Life Forever". Iqbal is empowering us by whispering us with secrets of soul.

تراجوہرہے نُوری، پاک ہے تُو   فنــروزغ دِیدۂ افلاک ہے تُو

"Pure in nature thou art, thy nature is light;
Thou art the star in the firmament"

Iqbal is again echoing the Divine message for mankind. Man, who has agreed to be a product of evolution and has forgotten any higher role assigned to him. Man, who has given all his strings to worldly desires that only fulfills the appetite of material body. Man, who is sinking into depth of illusion of matter. Iqbal invites them to primitive message of Lord. Reminding Man that your essence is light. You are a product of Divine spark which gives energy to this universe. Man's glow is pure and quintessence reality of this galaxy. Man's radiance illuminates the universe. Revealing that Man is pure. Further Iqbal added that Man is the blue-eyed of the holy skies. Man is the star among the stars. Man has been nurtured as most favored entity of the universe.

ترے صید زبوں ہیں افرشتہ خو

"*Thy preys are the nymphs and the angels bright*"

Iqbal reminds mankind, which is lost in aisles of worldly affairs, that Angels (and virgins of Heaven) are prey of your mind. Man, as a hunter, leads the universe and being privileged as the chosen entity of universe; he preys and hunts supernatral creatures. Thus, supernatutal entities are nothing but construct in human mind. Reflecting that consciousness is adobe of most holy ideas and entities. Ranking Man as a hunter or the leader of all forms of beings.

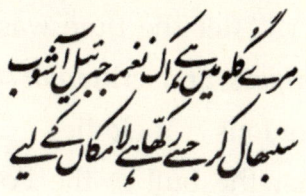

"I am saving a song for the Place-less Realm —
A song that could shake even the trusty Gabriel"

Before going into explanation of this verse, it is important to mention that why being poet is a privileged position in mankind. Though there are so many occupations available, yet poets are called to be unacknowledged legislators of the world. As metaphorically explained by Kierkegaard in his work Either/Or, that once upon a time there was a King Phil Arius. He had a metallic bull in which he used to punish offenders by putting them in it and burning fire underneath the bull's belly. Criminals would burn in it and would cry for help and mercy. Sounds of cry and mercy would make King uncomfortable, thus an advisor installed a whistle on the mouth of Bull; the source of cry and whimper. After the flute was placed, the cries of offenders and criminals were turned into harmonious melodies. Kierkegaard explained that the bull is the Poet and cries turned into sweet melodies are Poetry. Thus, poets carry the pain of mankind and turn into meaningful rhythms. So, we all can bear the life. As for absurdist writers, if the existence is absurd and bizarre then it's only poets who make meaning out of this pain. As said by a sage; when a broken-heart poet writes a poem, it mends hearts of hundreds. Poet burns his heart, spends sleepless nights to give us a lullaby so we can have sweet dreams. Certainly, poets have helped us to survive the crisis of existence in toughest days.

In this verse, Iqbal takes on his role of a poet to write the painful story of mankind. Taking birth, moving ahead with hope and passing by into infinity. Iqbal puts forward the chronicle of mankind, a tale of astonishment, finding meaning and reducing absurdity. Still connecting with the Lord, believing in Him and bearing pain.

Iqbal writes in this verse about the pain in his poetry while defending the case of the Man. He further adds that his poetry can even make Gabriel (AS) cry. Gabriel (AS) will also feel the pain of mankind who are left alone in this cage of space-time. But Iqbal declares that he has kept that one special song for space-less realms where he will see the God. There he would put forward his sad melody which would sensitize even Angels about the tragedy of the Man and they would sob while listening to the words of Iqbal.

Angel's Reply to Man

-

Diagnosis of Man's Decadence

Couplets used in this work are mostly borrowed from Iqbal's work *Gabriel (AS) Wing*. It would not be an honest review if we do not take Angels' view in this work. Iqbal addressed mankind from words of Angels also. Iqbal's book *Gabriel (AS) Wing* has a poem titled *Song of the Angel*. In this poem, Angels spoke about the deviant behaviour of mankind. What has made mankind as a chance-being, a product of evolution or nothing but a feeble body which may die today or tomorrow. Angels have addressed God. How most precious creation of God is merely a matter in motion now. How Man has lost the prestigious position which was endowed to them. Man, who was the co-creator of the universe, who had to lead the universe out of crisis of existence, who had to explore the dark matter, who had to make the universe a moral symbol, is himself lost in the fight of ID and Ego. Man, the archetype of perfection, is caught by moments of absurdity. Other reasons of fall are elaborated by the Angels. Thus, Iqbal looking at fall of Adam, looking at man captivated by mediocre agendas of life, held the pen on behalf of Angels and wrote to God.

In this book, we have read how Iqbal advocated case of Man in front of God and introduced Man's pain to supernatural beings. Original Sin or Adam eating the apple in heaven, gave birth to this worldly life, which is a compound of tears and joy, thus martyrdom of mankind has given life to this experience. Man has chosen mundane life in a feeble body, with a Machiavellian brain and passionate heart. Man has given colors to the canvas of existences. Man's return to God is cherished rather than that of Angels, Man's prayer to God are considered to be powerful than wings of Angels. But since the decay of Man's holy position and becoming a prisoner to economic life, Angels are now speaking to God.

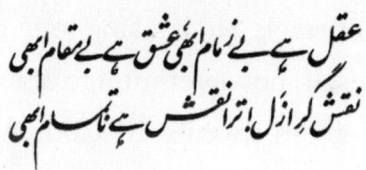

"As yet the Reason is unbridled, and Love is on the road:

O Architect of Eternity! Your design is incomplete"

It's Angels' turn to show the decadence of Man who was blessed with rationality and passion, who was blessed with heart and brain. Angels are putting forward their observation to God that though You blessed Man with the tool of rationality, yet Man's mind is not in his control rather these thoughts are astray; they are not using reason to create wonders but to create further menace. Man was bestowed with feeling of love, which made Abraham (AS) to jump in fire, Moses (AS) to walk through sea, Jesus (AS) to take the cross with smile, and Hussain (AS) to stand alone in Karbala. Ancestors of Man left reason dumbfounded with their intuitive decisions powered by love for you God, but now he is off-track. He is using love to possess more of himself, however mirage of love was to let-yourself-go in infinity of God. Angels are calling God as Prime Designer; Oh! you Eternal Architect, design of your supreme creation, i.e. Man, is left incomplete. Because Man is astray from the road which had to take him back to infinity and eternity. Road which had scents of heaven and sights of galaxies but Man has left the road.

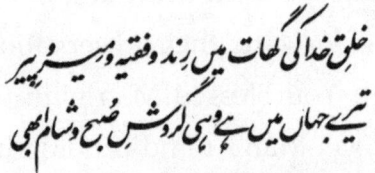

"Drunkards, jurists, princes and priests all sit in ambush upon Your common folk:
The days in Your world haven't changed as yet."

In the beginning of this work, we have clearly highlighted that rescuing Man from the crisis was one major goal of Iqbal. Iqbal was reintroducing Man bearing central position in the world. However, Angels are protesting that may it be drunkard or the judge, the rich aristocrats, or religious mentors, they all are misleading your simple men. People being on opposite poles, all are deceiving the Man.

Iqbal has shared a similar thought in his work *Call of the Marching Bell*:

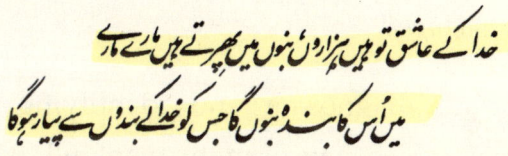

There had been many lovers of God, who appeared on earth, claiming the love of God, devoting themselves for His remembrance. However, for Iqbal, his mentor will be the one who has devoted himself for the service for mankind. Iqbal clearly criticized those Sufis/Saints, who isolate themselves from the community to search God. For Iqbal, a real Sufi/Saint finds God among the men. As God is nearer to men than their jugular vein.

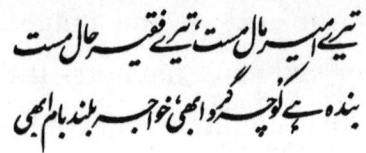

"Your rich are too unmindful, Your poor too content —
The slave as yet frets in the street, the master's walls are still too high"

Angels are diagnosing and identifying the dilemmas which have caught mankind. Man, the creature of perfection, is encircled by worldly affairs now. Rich people of land are intoxicated by the power of their wealth. Possessions have made them blind and they are carefree to pain of others. On the contrary, the poor class is satisfied and contented with the way they are living. They are oppressed by the rich class and affluent, yet the poor souls consider it to be the Will of God. Though poor should stand against oppression and may march for equality. But they assume this material poverty a Will of God or a chance to be mystic. It is a deception, says Iqbal.

In second part of the couplet, Iqbal in words of Angels, inform God that people living on opposite poles are blind from each other's miseries. Servants wander the streets and are finding a small place for shelter; the affluent ones, on the other hand, are raising fences high. The community is dividing. Man coming from single source has been divided into classes and they are not concerned about each other anymore. Gift of empathy, feeling for other, shedding tears in pain for other, not eating until your neighbour can eat, all these gifts have been lost by the Man. And now Man is standing alone intoxicated by his ego and wealth. He has lost the message of Iqbal that true mentor is the one: "There are thousands of God's Lovers, who are roaming in the wilderness. I shall adore the one who will be the lover of God's people."

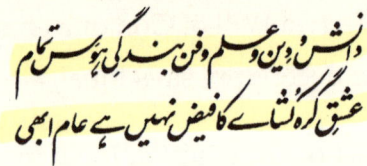

"Learning, religion, science and art are all means to fulfill lust: The grace of Love – the redeemer – is not as yet bestowed upon all"

Iqbal unveils the mystery of decadence of mankind. Mankind's aim of excelling in Science and Arts is not to know reality but to redeem personal ego. The goal is to satisfy one's ego. Goal is to look taller among masses. Knowledge, science, and arts are just working meals that human ego is devouring to grow itself taller. Here, ego isn't the ego as Will, but as selfish narcissistic desire. Iqbal considers religious men to be equally guilty in this task. Knowledge is not to know but to become; knowledge is not to memorize various facts but to be humble with the treasure of wisdom. Knowledge is the power which made Socrates cry "I know nothing, I know nothing". Iqbal mentions the panacea to all these ailments in next part i.e. Love. But Angels are concerned that love has not been unveiled on mankind yet. Love which prepares you to be a symbol of your loved one. Love which helps you kill your ego, as in one room only one ego should exist and that should be of my beloved. In love, absence has presence. By removing personal ego, Man embraces the infinite ego and walks out of selfish terrain of ME.

Iqbal quoted a similar verse in his book Call of the Marching Bell in poem "Reason & Heart".

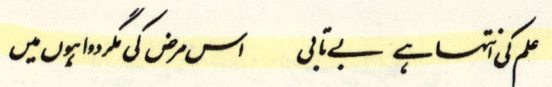

"Attaining the ultimate in knowledge only makes one restless –
I am the cure for that malady"

Knowledge is a process standing on pillars of refutation and evolution. The process moves forward at snail-pace. However, Man's life slips every second. We live in dilemma to know incremental knowledge which fulfills my existence at earth. On the other hand, I should also know the ultimate reality, as my life could end any day without a prior caution. Thus, Love cures all; the worries, the anxiety, the uncertainty, all are attended by love. While reason questions its already known knowledge, love hugs the reality and walks back.

Iqbal further speaks about the importance of love in last verse of the poem i.e. Song of Angels.

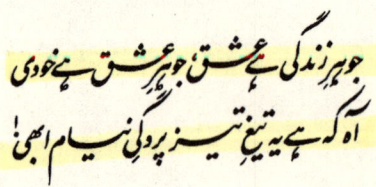

"The essence of Life is Love, the essence of Love is the self;
Alas! This cutting sword as yet rests in the sheath!"

What is life? Moment of love. What is love? To find one true self. As Khwaja Meer Dard wrote in his Persian work: "Love is the only season of spring in the garden of life". Taking off all the covers, removing all the fake layers of existence, we find ourselves. That is only possible until we fall in love, until we beat reason with intuition, until we find a zone of consciousness beyond rationality. As Rumi said: "Beyond good and evil (poles of rationality), there is an island; Come there, you will find God." Reason is house of possessions, may it be material or ideas. Only love teaches to let go, to give yourself back to the Grand-Ego. What if your weak personal ego is standing between you and your God? What if your material understanding is the barrier between you and the Lord? You have to learn to unlearn to see with these eyes. If you want to see Him, raise yourself up, do master creations, be a scholar of science, read philosophy. Once you have exhausted your all mental faculties, then knock on the door of heart that I am still thirsty, I am in crisis of existence, I am rusting, life is appearing more absurd, come and save me, oh love! Angels have advised mankind to be the barrier of Love and Will, to resolve the universe.

In last, Angels sang that Man has the ultimate weapon of Love and Will, which he has not unleashed yet. He has been caught in labyrinth of rationality, logic, and reason. Though he had the sword of Love, which would have liberated Man from all form of anxieties. Sadly, this sword is still kept in the sheath. Man has not unveiled or used the greatest of faculty i.e. Love.

Angel's Advice to Man before bidding Farewell from Heaven

Song of Angels had some key-learning for the mankind, so they can identify the causes of their decline. That song appears as a diagnosis of Man of this age, who is suffering from the intoxication of wealth and ego. They gain knowledge to hail their personal self, and they work extra to accumulate wealth. Later, we find another poem in Iqbal's book i.e. Gabriel Wing in which Angel bid farewell to Adam (First Prophet/ Archetypal man) from Heaven. Thus, this poem is a reflection of miracles which God bestowed mankind with. Angels are acknowledging Man's constructive role in this universe as he has been blessed with most important attributes. In Song of Angel, Angels are identifying the causes of decadence of Man but in this poem i.e. *Angels bid farewell to Adam from Heaven*, Angels are looking at Man in his virgin state. Man, which has not been corrupted by his ego. Man, who is stepping down on Earth to change the world of matter into moral. Angels are bidding farewell to God's supreme-creation. Thus, Angels are praising Man in first verse of this poem:

عطا ہوئی ہے تجھے روزوشب کی بیتابی   خبر نہیں کہ تو خاک کی ہے یا کہ سیمابی

"You have been given the restlessness of Day and Night,
We know not whether you are made of clay or mercury."

Universe with its living and non-living things is passive, however, only Man is the active vicegerent of God. All other beings are enslaved by innate habits. Thus, only Man has that restlessness to explore the universe. Thus, Angels are recognizing Man as an active phenomenon of universe who is about to take his role as Caliph of God. Blessed with restlessness, blessed with power of abstraction. Angels further confess that they are not sure that this Man is a Being made by clay or mercury. Though Man is existing in carrier of clay and sand, yet he has a soul which rises like mercury. Man can't fly but certainly his ideas can. Man has limits but his ideas are boundless. Man has boundaries but his passion can take him to skies.

سنا ہے خاک سے تیری نمود ہے، لیکن   تری سرشت میں ہے کوکبی و مہتابی

"We hear you are created from clay,
But in your nature is the glitter of Stars and
Moon"

Subsequently, Angels are enlightening Adam (man in his pure form) about essence of his Being. Though you are made of clay and bounded by a mortal body, but you are the only light of this universe. Your essence holds the energy and light of celestial bodies. Man is the only subject of this universe which allows other objects to exist. Man's observation helps any object to qualify for existing. Thus, Man may not consider himself as biological being, rather Man is a spiritual being having energy to touch the zenith.

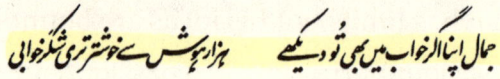

"Your sleep would be preferable over much wakefulness

If you could behold your own beauty even in a dream!"

Angels are shaking the Man, with their advises, so Man may not consider himself as a biological being and pass away the spiritual life captivated by the bounds of material body. Though sleeping is considered to be a passive activity, in which mediocre man is left on the disposal of subconscious mind. Yet if Man may actualize his position, if Man would realize his real self, if Man would acknowledge himself as the supreme-creation of God, then his sleep is even better than thousands of wakeful hours. Thus, Man once actualizing himself, becomes a symbol of God though he isn't uttering a word.

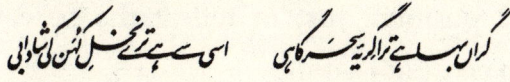

"Your morning sighs are invaluable
For they are the water to your ancient tree"

Night is much darker than the word Night.
Night is much darker than the darkness. When
darkness veils the visible world, it's only the
Man who wakes up to recall his Creator. Night
desires to open up the day, but only Man wakes
up in darkest hours and give the call (Azaan) for
day's beginning. Thus, Angels are reminding
Man that he is the carrier of spiritual message.
Man has been cut off and is on a distance from
his Beloved, from his Creator, thus Man is
longing to be with Him, Man cries to see the
Beloved. Fear of God is not of a tyrant master,
rather fear of God is fear of losing the most
beautiful lover. Hence, this cry and sob in
memory of God turn this body of clay into gold.
The ancient tree is referred to the time when
Man was with God in paradise. Now, far away,
longing of Man could help him reclaim that

exalted position. Just to reflect the power of human cry, Eliot said:

> *"This is the way the world ends*
> *Not with a bang but a whimper"*

بڑی نوا سے ہے بے پردہ زندگی کا ضمیر

کہ تیرے ساز کی فطرت نے کی ہے پردہ نوائی

> *"Your melody unravels the secret of life*
> *For it is Nature that has attuned your organ"*

In the last verse of the poem, Iqbal recalls Man as the only active sound which translates life in the universe. Man has been gifted with passion, words, poetry, tragedy which gives life to the lifeless universe. Universe is nothing but matter, waiting to be explored by the Man. But for this, Man has paid the cost. To gain this life, Man has paid the cost in form of pain & sorrows of existence. Pain and sorrows are parcels of this mortal body. Man picked up that responsibility, Man has been martyred to give life and meaning to this universe. Thus, Man has been chosen by the nature to play the divine tune. Divine tune? Divine tune of life, movement, excelling, creating, and writing. In Divine orchestra, Man is the only chosen organ that translates life. This deaf and dumb universe, made up by matter, has an organic being that has the keys to immortality. Man has been bestowed to take up the role of vicegerent and caliph of God. Melodies stirred by the organ of Man has turned this world into museum of wonders. By great work of arts and science, Man has tried his best to increase the productivity of this universe.

Final Words

Man has given meaning to himself and this matter universe. Man has carried the weight of free-will, reason, and passion when no other creation was ready to pick it up. Man has martyred himself. Sadly, Man, who has been through the tragedy, was left alone. May it be economic system, religion or a social system, individual was left unattended. Yuval Noah further added that Man of this age is feeling to be irrelevant. As if this existence is an unwanted load. Crawling like Kafka's insect, from one wall to another, waiting for the end. Globalization in name of humanism is a project of de-humanization. Man has been stripped off from his innate qualities & differences. Man has been called to stand in queue of normality which has been defined by the powerful entities. Differences & individual's beauty is compromised in name of global struggle. Myths, totems, and norms, made through centuries, have been erased and everyone is called for global values. Thus, Iqbal undertook an effort in Gabriel Wing to restore Man's position in universe. The position which was lost in different epochs of time. Tyrants in different forms appeared in history to make Man irrelevant of his position. Pushing him to be a passion-less soldier or asking him to work on assembly lines for dream of a capitalist. Man, in history, was left as a biological being surviving on grounds of Darwin's theory. Iqbal has tried to echo God's message to the ordinary man. Man as the caliph, Man as the vicegerent, Man as the co-creator, Man as the flute, Man as the sword, Man as the lover of God. This effort of Iqbal would help Man to be mindful of his existence and find the bigger role in this ephemeral time. As Iqbal wrote in his magnum opus i.e. Cordova Mosque:

ہاتھ ہے اللہ کا بندۂ مومن کا ہاتھ

غالب و کار آفریں، کار کشا، کار ساز

"The might of the man of faith is the might of the Almighty:
Dominant, creative, resourceful, consummate."

Editor's Note

In spite of Iqbal's intense philosophical earnestness, he is considered a poet substantially. In his poetic universe Angels hold a vast place clearly but Man is that part of the universe which is greater than the whole.

Writing is surely an enormous act of courage but reading it, is nothing short of a valiant act. Besides, when writer like Khurram Ellahi is writing and that too about Iqbal; you have to muster up enough courage to gather the write-ups that give so much to think about. Certainly, I cannot tell you about the taste of the book, this you have to find on your own. However, I can assure you that it's not the clichéd one-time read; you have to pick it up more than once and the morsels would taste different each time yet the recipe remains the same.

I profoundly thank him for entrusting me with this beautiful piece which I get to read prior to anyone. An honor for me, indeed.

Thank you, Khurram Bhai, for being a disguised-angel whom I can look upon to, always.

Sabeen Mustafa

Author's Profile

Khurram Ellahi is a PhD Scholar of Human Resource Management, who completed his MS and academic career with multiple Gold Medals. He has been working as motivational speaker while capitalizing on his love for literature and natural sciences. He has been mastering to amalgamate scattered knowledge at one place, he has also been delivering lectures on how one science or subject can resolve the problem of other science or subject e.g. Physics and Poetry. Hence helping students and trainees to encompass knowledge in totality rather than in boxes.

Khurram has various research papers published in realm of fiction and management sciences; Quran and Workplace Diversity, Servant Leadership, Leadership from poetic work of Iqbal etc. Khurram has completed first book from Pakistan which looks at Business & Management through lens of poetry, named Managers as Little Prince.

He is also doing a philosophical TV show on PTV Home titled Nukta.

MANAGERS AS LITTLE PRINCE

In this book, Khurram Ellahi has used the novel The Little Prince written by Saint-Exupéry to attend the long-lasting dilemmas of Business & Management. This is first of its kind endeavor from Pakistan. New thinking approach has been introduced to attend the old problems of management. Book also looks at conventional approach of attending those dilemmas and how thinking like Little Prince can help Managers and how poetry & fiction has already influenced physics, psychology and other fields of knowledge.